The Terrible Wife

TERRY ANN THAXTON is an award winning writer. She teaches creative writing at the University of Central Florida in Orlando. Her poems and essays have appeared or are forthcoming in *Gulf Coast*, *Main Street Rag*, *Futurecycle*, *Connotation Press*, *The Missouri Review*, *Fourth River*, *Cold Mountain Review*, *Teaching Artist Journal*, and other literary journals.

Also by Terry Ann Thaxton from Salt

Getaway Girl (Salt, 2011)

The Terrible Wife

by

TERRY ANN THAXTON

SALT

CROMER

PUBLISHED BY SALT PUBLISHING
12 Norwich Road, Cromer Norfolk NR27 0AX, United Kingdom

© Terry Ann Thaxton, 2013

Salt Publishing 2013

Printed and bound in the United States by Lightning Source Inc

Typeset in Swift 9.5 / 13

ISBN 978 1 84471 916 7 paperback

1 3 5 7 9 8 6 4 2

for Don, always

Contents

Acknowledgements

I am grateful to the editors of the following journals, in which some of these poems, often in earlier versions, first appeared: *Apalachee Review, Avatar, Berkeley Poetry Review, Cimarron Review, Earth's Daughters, Flyway, Foliate Oak, Forge, FutureCycle, Gulf Coast: A Journal of Art and Literature, South Carolina Review, WomenArts Quarterly*.

I owe more than these words to Shaindel Beers, Lisa Roney, Don Stap for reading these poems, from early drafts to final editing. Love to Adam for always writing.

I would also like to thank Chris Hamilton-Emery at Salt for his support and for all of the beautiful books.

Part I. *Free Girls*

Free Girls

On Oleander Street in Sarasota, Florida,
my best friend—my cousin, my confidant—

shared a room with her know-it-all sister,
Debbie. Every Saturday I spent the night,

my right shoulder to Janet's left, on her twin
bed. We pretended to be boy and girl.

The skin of my hand on her face; the skin of her
hand on my arm. Instead of kissing, we

narrated, but always the boy wanted the girl, always
the boy cooled her skin. He chased the girl

through the sky, and when Debbie came in
from being out with her newest boyfriend, she

called us stupid little girls. "Leave my makeup alone,"
she'd say. But she did not know the curses

we had placed on her in the darkness:
Girls who stay out late cause the moon to fall

into their bellies; the black night of family is like
turning the last page of a true story.

Instead, we crossed our fingers beneath
the sheet, and said, "So sorry, Madame. We'll obey."

On Sunday we rose as new women.

Janet has her own children now, and she walks them
to school, and does not think of me.

She and I have slept next to many men
since we swam out of her house. She does not know

of the years I spent wanting to live in her house,
where her mother allowed us to be girls, where two girls

secretly made up dances though they were not
supposed to — it was a sin; yes, we were noticed,

but only by the voices on the radio. *Get yourselves
outta this house,* we'd hear. Always the bicycles

called for us. We rode through the streets surrounding
her house: we wore no makeup. We flew

through intersections. Free girls. We did not know
the true stories of the men we would find,

how our skin would bruise from their hands.

The Beach

Of course the girl doesn't talk to boys.
Her tiny breasts are, however, hopeful.
Last night she thought his hand meant he loved her—skunk
out the car window, sour milk, a hard
she'd never touched before, radio, the dark—
and in the van, even though her mother was driving her
to church, her brothers sitting next to you,
everyone singing with the Beatles
on the radio, "All you need is love,"
his hand reached between the seat and the window,
from behind her, put it where he wanted to.

He whispered: "touch me."
She thought, Where is my promise ring? She imagined
her fingers as five golden rings choking
his penis. And now he sits in the shade
of another girl—the girl he asked
to go steady with him.
If only he had asked her to like him,
she would have slung mud in his eyes.

At the beach, children swim out under waves.
The girl digs a hole. Buries herself.

She hopes that one day he will
not be in her dreams, just as she hopes
sand will creep over her. She imagines, someday, climbing
the distant mountains, sensing voices
behind her. But drenched in salt water, she lies
still. The other girls have gone up the beach now,
laughing. She does not know yet that down the street,
after many years, she will want to die.

She will tear at her clothes. She will rise from a nightmare and declare: "I'll never be happy."
He was a boy. She must have wanted it after all.

Girls of the 1960s Grow Up and Get Married

We march out into the trees
or fly off our balconies looking for a man,
any man.

We open our windows and let the light in,
then think of ourselves
as flowers in our own pockets.

We wonder how today happened.

Here we are, gathering sex toys
in rooms filled with pillows.

No one understands our writing
or our hands on the teapot.
The grass has dried
like our hands on the cup
of water, covering the napkin.

We walk out from under the clouds
into the boxes beneath the trees.
We ask, "Why can't we come along?"

What if I am the only woman about to leave town,
and the shame I felt in the field
is still aiming for the sky of my youth.

The Brick Walkway

The theory is that saving bricks
from the old walkway
could be an imitation of someone

else's life. For this you'd need
to chisel your name into my

forehead, or look into a mirror
to guess my name. Sometimes tossing

a ball is hazardous.
Sometimes the dandelions
want to scream.

Sometimes my hands commit
themselves to famine.

If I made a tapestry to sing my life
I'd be the eye waiting for trees to collide.

This world is slippery when it asks
me for my fantasy life
or when I am casting my net

across the floor where we live like
chameleons waiting for rapture.

The Photograph of My First Child

The man slapped his future onto mine.
There was no one like him:
Many times he held onto my hair or burned a blouse.

He persuaded the trees to take my clothes,
forced the house to capture my arms in its wooden walls.

He kept ordering me: a book to open, my mouth to close.
Come here, he kept repeating. *Stop.*
This fist is closed. (As if I didn't know.) And then

he blew up: became a black balloon tilted in the sky.
I wanted the roads to pull him into the center line, but it took
more than fifty wishes (and twenty years) to get him

out of the stew he had made for me—
inside were his words: *bitch, slut,*
crybaby, good-for-nothing. I never stopped

looking up. I still see his body, firing at me
after he returned from fishing, and I imagine
the unborn child
that he punched out of me
has never stopped
hunting him. It was a photograph of the fetus

inside a plastic bag that he'd thrown onto the coffee table.

The curse of the sky revealed itself to me, here, at this house
next to the dirt road, where nothing
is buried.

Wife-in-Training

I found a family once, cutting down
a Christmas tree, and as a gift to myself
I imagined myself as the wife,
part of that family. I followed them
from the lot—my own little self-help course
in how-to-follow-without-being-noticed—
to their gated house.

I've always wanted to be a wife.
There have been years of soup and salad and fresh
tea. There have been days when I've eaten
no candy, only fresh fruit. I've never smoked.
Spirits of ex-husbands

sit down and take names from my TV, and I confess
that once, maybe two or three times, I lit a cigarette
and relished the flame. In the supermarket
details are scarce. I never follow the right path,
never following the aisles in order,
but I end up in the checkout lane:
as if I am a real wife.

& After

I will construct my final resting place,
like a solitary wasp, out of sand and ash.

I will speak of my regrets: my wild, early,
and lousy demonstration of motherhood.

I will, no doubt, hold onto my inability
to put things back where I found them,

my inability to speak in public, and my yelling
at the neighbor, whose dog barked all weekend.

I will never let go of getting down on my knees
in a gesture of sarcasm, to beg the neighbor

for her royalty's forgiveness. I will hold onto
my forgetfulness, my inability to close

the doors to the laundry room, the week
or more it took me to complete a single load

of laundry. I will remember my mother:
an argument against becoming a wife.

I will recall the years she reminded me of my hair,
how it falls into my eyes the way it does, and how

I would never become a wife a man would keep.

Part II.   *The Men of My Dreams*

House on the Creek

future: wrap-around porch, wood
floors, antique furniture, a lion's
claw on the dining table, two
people staring at each other
like white walls that hunger for
music

now: two kayaks, bromeliads
brick walkway to the dock
pine sap and a few flowers, no dogs
or children, the dirt, a creek
and a dock, the fireplace,
her glass, roses, goldenrod—

then: a few birds, and a dark creek

My First Rental

On the edge of Highway 41
I sat on the steps and imagined which cars
might stop to rescue me, wondered if I could trade
the jalousie windows for a guitar and become
a rock star. I waited every day
for his body to warn me
of arrival. Every day I cooked for him.
Every day I went outside and looked up
into the trees. Often I dared myself
to grab the cast iron pot.
The days he did not come home
he was either fishing or at Bob's,
getting high. The sink was never clean.
His rifle announced
his arrival. One day the house will no longer exist,
and I will not be able to find the exact spot
where I buried my escape plan. Instead I'll drive
to where his mother still lives, sit out front
in my car, daring myself to knock on the door and tell her
what he did to me. Then I'll drive to my new,
comfortable home, where no one calls to ask how
I managed to stay in that place. It was a tiny, rotting
house where two people
learned to hate. Sometimes I think I hear
the road just outside that little house, reminding me
what happened in the years after I left:
the bulldozers, and now, in its place, storage units
where people leave possessions
they do not wish to keep or give away.

The Preacher's Wife

He is kind. They have been married for five years,
but she no longer wants
to be saved. His smile keeps telling her he's

comforting the dead, but really he's watching
skirts for hire in dark rooms,
hung in all their glory, while she totes a child

through rhymes. This wins her a riot
and the water shivers
away from this life that she thought she wanted.

She lets her hair stand on end, then her dress stinks.
She and the crows in the yard scheme,
but suddenly, the preacher ends it all

by whining. Rumor insists she have a knife
in her hand, instead she finds a gift:
warblers swerving in tribes, and when she opens

their bedroom door an old wound
opens. The birds wait outside.

Don't Marry Your Brother-in-Law

Then one day, he called me aside, out of the group
of others who'd been helping us keep our secret,
and even though I knew this was a dream, I knew
he wanted to tell me something:
Marry me, marry me, marry me.

                                 He's already married, I thought,
but still I agreed.
                    We took our babies from blister packs,
one at a time, as if popping little pills
    into our lives, but still he wanted
his current wife to think their baby was still alive—
                our pill baby would be the stand-in,
but the babies were pre-packaged and they'd live
    only a day or so.

It would be best, we decided, to kill the fabricated baby
before his wife found out it wasn't real, and that's when
                I was glad we'd only killed one baby so far
at a grocery store checkout counter.

                And then, there came about a new baby
we could keep. We named him Jackson. It wasn't like I was cheating
    on my husband—
he wasn't part of this life I was living.

But even in this dream, I try to remind myself I am already married,
shouldn't marry my brother-in-law,
                    no matter how much
he said he loved me, no matter how firm his ass.
Our pre-packaged baby lived and we were happy.
                The baby grew. The baby shopped for purses.
I transferred him from one

middle school to another, and finally agreed
to buy the big purse he'd found
                              which I would need for travel
since I was certain my brother-in-law/husband would soon
    grow tired of me, as all the others had,
                    would want his old life back—
and Jackson and I would have to find a way
                                    out of this dream.

"Dragonfly With Red Wings"
Joan Miro, Oil on Canvas

I told myself to sleep
or get inside a car again— another man.
I beat
my fists on the pavement

could see them all
waving their fingers at me. I wanted to be
part of a wall of women dancing
water falling from the sky or a fountain.

Sometimes the Good Luck Tree,
sometimes the Red Sister,
like a woodpecker chasing away blue jays
from the feeder, sprouts a brush
when I'd rather have sweet arms.

People do not look
at each other for fear of dropping
the bag of groceries into the sand.
And what if a tiny patch
of blue appears or a path with several
moons at the end?

What if box means box
bird means bird?
What if the oak trees continue
looking like broken people?

They don't mean anything.
It's not that I did not
exist, but rather perhaps I have been
filled with unidentifiable flowers

and am still lingering
at the store where I stood
as a girl
where a mask (or was it a star?)
of the future hung far above my head.

The Night I Married Jasper Jax

"And he took a woman with him. It's so damn typical."
        — JASPER JAX, on the American soap opera *General Hospital*

We had to switch hotel rooms, but Jax had already unbuttoned
his shirt, revealed his soap opera body. Sure his hair
was a mess, but at the wedding,

I was in my gown, a few ruffles,
and even though I'd bought it at Wal-mart
it stood out. Someone chanted African songs
from down the unseen hallway
and a woman danced instead of a flower girl.

The only part I did not like was the poster presentation
of my previous four marriages. I didn't want everyone to see
how cute my first husband was,
how stupid I'd been with husband number 2,
how husband number 3 had grown fat. And where was
husband number 4? Why didn't he get

a poster? The poster for husband number 1
included a video, and someone at the wedding had seen
him recently. Told me he'd widened in his age. Good,
I thought. Someone that cute should get fat.

And then our hotel room was a public place,
the wedding guests wanted to see our bed, which
is when they applauded. It took a while to convince
them that the reception was somewhere else,

down a long road. My sister drove me and a few guests
through mountains. She kept swerving too far

off the side. Someone next to me, not Jax,
kept yelling at her to slow down, to stay on the road.
"This works," she kept repeating. "This works."

Last thing I remember was a big turn in the road,
Jax back there in another car, wondering where
his new bride was headed, and the road, endless,
all of my husbands far, far behind.

Lost Hunger

There was another life, and I waited with my
lost skirt—its rumpled pleats. For days—no, for months—

or was it years? I hunted for food outside the window
of the abandoned trailer where I camped with my hunger.

That was the summer I carried forty dollars and my baby
from Florida to Texas with a man. I was the first

to wake up each day. I learned to hide inside
with my baby and his blanket, under the imagined window,

the hole in the wall with no screen. And now,
that vine of lost hunger is twenty-five years old

and I lie inside my wooded yard, a real lake behind it.
The sky closes in toward a street light. The man is now

distant and small. He does not appear in any pictures
from the past, nor in the walls or posts of this house.

In the dark, outside, there are some posts: white, separating
the porch light from the ginger plants of my present

and the truth of the suburbs, the truth of the road finally
being paved along the graveyard of houses. I am the only

proof that hunger has flown out of my life. And here,
only I am to blame for the ending.

The Cold Rising of the Sun

I was emptying the jar of water into the moon light.
It would have shined all night above the house
where barred owls call, desperate to mate in the trees,
had I believed in it. Female on one side,
calling,
You look at me, you,
You look at me, you.
The male on the other side, saying back,
You look at me, you look at me.

In daylight, I carry my silver pot, hear smooth
singing, but always the female waits
until the male's voice falls
short. She's never sure he's calling only for her.
Too often, she's flown down

into the dust of this earth. I tried to find him. I pulled
my trowel out of the sand. I did not look
at the blue jays and cardinals nor bother with the storm
that scattered. I waited for more light.
My legs became daisies, those flowers with long
yellow dots of definitive fear. The female owl cries

each day before dusk. I want to ignore
the mourning doves whose voices make me think
of past lovers. I should know what is true.

She must have been amazing, the woman
my husband fell in love with and married. He met her
when she still felt young, though dust-covered.
Sometimes he remembers to hold her, to hold me,
as though I'm still a little girl, afraid
I'll be left calling for him on a branch,

afraid he'll hear another voice, and go a different direction,
and of course, I'll wait,
crazy girl that I am, through dinner, through dark,
even through the cold rising of the sun the next morning.

The Terrible Wife

Something is dragging me
into a room, screened in—a dream
in which I am about to have
an affair. I run my fingers
through the other man's hair while
my husband circles
the building, and I realize
we're in a picnic shelter,
like the one my family
went to when I was
a girl, at the state park, where
a friend of mine jumped
into the pond at dusk and
was killed by an alligator.

The room laughs, and I kneel
in the corner, curl into a ball,
like a hog-nose snake and hope
my husband will not
see me. He keeps his face
turned away
from the screen, as if
he is refusing to return
phone calls of long lost
friends. I stay in
the corner until the
man I'm with is handed
a note along with a flashlight,
the message: *shine the flashlight*
in the corner so you can see
who's there, and it's me,
of course, still huddled there
as if I am mud
tracked in on the back

porch, but it's more
like I'm standing
naked in a field
of pond apple. I go back
to rubbing the man's temples,
and we both realize there are school
projects to be completed
by morning, and he helps
my brother while I help my son,
and then I am in my car
but I can't quite
catch the bullfrog that jumped in
beside me, so I go back
inside. I want to
stay here. I know the note
and flashlight were from
my husband who, now, obviously
knows about the affair, and I
think I should wake up,
end this thing, but right now
I want to be terrible.

Part III. *Where Things Lie*

Tractor Song

There are days my walking takes longer
and often it is when crows
are laughing at my shoulders
or when a truck arrives in an unknown driveway or
the horse at the corner stomps the ground

a tractor mows in a reluctant field
and it is as if childhood has taken my place
and my old self leaves me there

I knew I could easily become
the woman holding
the apple in the horse's mouth

or the woman waiting to hear
the Bible of her childhood again

as I grew
I coaxed myself toward this new place
these roads I walk every day
in dust and in mud and even in rain

~

Back then my goal was to not make anyone angry
it was the steel envelope of a fist
the iron balloon
I disliked

all this time and only one man's hand
has been a feather   still
I remember singing on a tractor
Gospel hymns   *Trust and obey, for there's no other way*
To be happy in Jesus, but to trust and obey

thinking no one could hear me sing those
songs I'd memorized on oak pews
in a church nowhere near these roads

where no one sees my hands
reaching for the feather that appeared one day

just as no one was there to watch me lift
my words into the water falling
into the rain

Haircut

Once when my husband left town for a week
I adopted a dog. She followed me
around the house, and even though
it wasn't a child I'd picked out
and taken to the store where I bought new toys, food,
and a bed; even though it wasn't a child who rode
in the back seat of my car, we returned her.
We had not discussed adopting a dog.
Instead, we signed papers, agreeing we'd never call to ask
whether the dog was adopted again or euthanized.
Weeks later when I left town for a business trip,
I returned home with a new haircut.
In the distance, the Indian Temple's chants
steamed through the trees, over saw palmettos,
across the dirt roads toward our barren house.
Even after my husband assured me
over and over that my hair was wickedly smart,
I dreamed I brought home two more dogs, hid them
from him, and an elephant—easier to hide,
only its gray trunk a problem. When I was a girl,
my cousin and I cut each other's hair.
We wanted "Shag" cuts, layers across the back. It was the
mid-'70s, cutting hair seemed easy enough. Two girls
with scissors. Lines stacked in our hair
like on pieces of notebook paper, lines so straight
you could write on them. The teacher
at the elementary school where I volunteer says
with my new haircut I look like Tina Turner,
cropped with highlights, and I dance for her:
"What's love got to do with it?" I don't tell her
what Tina and I share—how my first husband
held a gun to my head, how he demanded

we have children and then beat one of them out
of me. Instead the teacher and I laugh,
and the children tumble into the room
from lunch behind my back—their sweet dark heads
covered with cornrows, Zulu knots, braids,
locks, Bantus, extensions, finger waves, twists,
and weaves. They run their fingers through my
stringy never-stays-where-I-put-it hair.
These children are all hugs and pouts
and pictures they draw of me—
sometimes, in their drawings, my hair is yellow,
sometimes red, sometimes curly, sometimes
long. I'm there to write
with them. We are strangers, and soon
their stories become letters on the page,
and nothing else in me needs to be filled.

Rock Beneath Orange Tree

Carpenter ants, because they rather enjoy living
inside rotten wood, scattered when I lifted a rain-soaked
log from beneath ragweed. These rocks know to stay away
from the sky, prefer the earth: those smooth, land-boats,
maliciously sunken, spend a lifetime on or inside dirt,

and then there is my life:
the roofer who did not show today,
you calling to report that the airlines, again—that same
joke—lost your luggage, which is when

I thought: I could be that rock I moved today
to mow the grass, or the rock I did not move, sitting still
beneath the orange tree in the side yard, hoping
for the detainment of light in its false contentment,
with its one-way flight into soil.

Dusk: I wait for you to arrive home, and across the room,
the trees of our past, the birds you carried in your mouth
fly toward my hands.

Birdsong
after Birdsong *by Don Stap*

This is a portrait at dawn, your song, where lust holds
the same territory as the now absent northern flicker

the bottom of an imaginary lake or the ancient Douglas fir

Drumming serves the same function and points
the sound across some darkened trail marker

There is no going back though we are connected
to the recorder where you once mouthed *birdsong*

into nearby darkness so close

like someone working in his own wood shop
in the fall   here we might understand

the airplane overhead but if we were
the chestnut sided warbler it might be a ghost

or loose cluttering or trees that have now become dominant
Here we need to be cautious near the brown thrush

and this hypothetical hunt for a simpler song
still   between the songs of the blackbird

we can avoid silence while the hummingbird
though with swing song, dresses hurriedly

and tries everything males usually try—that flight
that is only a slip worked into his composition

about the lesson of boundaries somewhere
northeast of the city they wrapped

tinfoil around a red-breasted sapsucker fresh
from the nest at five days old. Someone reports warming

trends—on the surface it seems likely that several birds
will share songs though they were raised in isolation:

sparrows, buntings, chickadees,
wrens, thrashers, starlings,

and then it begins to look like a forest where it might be

more convenient for us to believe that they all exist
in a single place—where a bird's singing might impress

children (or lovers) who are just learning
to say the words, to say *mock-ing-bird*, bordering

years that have fallen into a thick cover
of glorious muddy roads—there is always an open song

even when the roads are dark even when the singing
is muffled even when the birds are silent

Sounds Coming Through Empty Sky

Not so far away from the quiet black needle rush and
the *oh come here* of red-winged blackbirds,
there were trucks I dodged to walk to the end
of the street where houses lined
the marsh road.

In his dream last night
I wanted to bring home two babies
but he would only agree to one.
Were they the two of us as infants
like the books on our shelves standing next
to each other? There's the story of my life
and the story of the last ten years of our life,
stories of the birds he followed,
sounds coming through empty sky
like the marsh today where, I know I am forever
alone no matter which man stands next to me.

I am invisible here
in the woods where there is nothing
between me and a few hours of walking
or sleeping or wandering off down
the street, where the sun is setting,
where I wait for my pockets to fill
with keys that will let me back
into my own life.

From a Cabin in Portal, AZ
(Population: 60)

We filled the bird bath each morning—
by noon: nothing. Nest of road runner.
Dust. The entire mountain range.
The street a leather tongue of dust,
losing itself behind the tires
of unseen cars. We became what whispers,
watching the Milky Way as if it would disappear
if we spoke. We were the dark, separating
the desert from our toes. I was the sheet
under which he slept. We gave each other
shape. He was the keeper
of feathers and rocks found among trees and
birds. He became my stillness. He called
for new birds. We had many walks in common,
forgetful of our past, unlit until the sky appeared
before us a new thing: a cloud of white dust.

Burden of Memory

One day you will lie on a boardwalk over marsh

you will hear a spring of blue-winged teal
rise from water like leaves of corn stalks
touching the wind.

The birds will tell you how much
they have lost in this life:
we can touch clouds
but, destined to the earth,
we cannot go beyond the sky
even on a clear day

you will remember that as a child
you lay in cornfields looking up, needing birds.

Where Things Lie

Silent, above the dulled green carpeting, which we call
our space, I run freely toward the door where you stand,

where you've raised your hand, as if you are my student,
the quiet boy in the back row, finally getting his chance.

It is our game—me in my study, you asking
me to come out to play. But this time I am almost certain

that if I call on you I will fall into the bleached
pond bottom outside, that you've come to tell me

you're ready to give away all of our plants to someone
you once left behind, someone you meant to bring with you

into the rest of your life, and now I'm simply a single flower
you want to push away. I see myself begin to float,

only to land at another place, separate from our raised beds.
It is you, as a young man, she wishes to take away, without me

noticing. Most times I'm certain we will never die,
but simply rise to the tops of trees for a short time, and then

become forever entangled in each other's limbs and leaves
and vines. But now you stand framed at the door,

and the light feels its way outside, and all I fear is that one day
I could lose your hand—the only boy's hand I want.

I do not want to give away our game, nor the sand, swishing
endlessly beneath our feet, which is white—

a quiet and complete landscape—and, for me, everything.

Part IV. *Trouble in Paradise*

Bougainvillea

Our plan was to mix the concrete to mount
an arbor for the bougainvillea
I'd planted next to the pine, its scattered
branches like my arms that, for years, had ached
for romance. Instead, it rained.

Drizzled as it is likely to do
in Florida, and like the interruption
of the rain, a letter appeared
in the mailbox,
from a woman—an old friend—to my husband,
begging him to come visit her
in another city.

In separate rooms
inside the house
we waited for
Florida sun again, which took days, and jealousy

waited with me like the thorns
on the bougainvillea, and when we drove
to the grocery store, at each stop light,
he told me how the woman from the past
is a blank journal entry from
thirty years ago. I think of the calendar

the new year just days old,
and the lattice I have woven into our
yard. But I cannot stop my mangled

thoughts. I am certain his heart did not leap
at the sight of me shoving the post-hole digger

into the ground
to make ready for the arbor
that would show visitors the way

to the butterfly island in our yard.
Back home, in my small room
where no one could see the many solstices
I have counted on knowing
that I am the only one. I imagined myself
to be the anonymous woman hanging backwards,
in a Gorey print between the branches

of a pine tree, hoping that the man
will catch her if she falls.
I imagined the two people in black
cloaks watching as the dog raises his chin
to take a letter from her hand,
but another woman
in white passes a note to one of the
people in black, but oh, how I, in my tiny room,

imagined myself hanging
upside down, how I want
the dog to take a letter from my hand
deliver it to my husband, asking for everything
I don't know how to ask, and then I imagined

a person in black
flying above me/her/the woman
with outstretched hands,
and the tree becomes
darkness and the path

circling all of them
rips the fantasy to lace. Perhaps none of us
will ever have what
we truly want. The dog is, of course, on a leash,

but the person holding him doesn't
seem to care if he comes along
or not, and it is oh so
important, the letter. I am holding onto it.

Trouble in Paradise: A Four Act Play

I. Open Curtain

These blinds are always open. In their veins
Florida is filled with grass like a tiled
green journal dotted with moss and pine
needles that have fallen during the rains.

There's nothing to say about her. She stains
my garden with an unlived story, glides
from a past to our present; her words hide
beneath leaves. I am jealous. But I'll hang

on like the sun in the summer solstice,
like saw palmetto buried in the woods—
a woodpecker that clings to the hollow

tree. Can't he see that she is a temptress
instead of an ancient and cherished book?
She's a room filled with poems I'll never know.

II. The Setting in the Trees

There's a room filled with poems she'll never know:
Florida polished green, its vines and shrubs,
burgundy toenails that I use to grab
his back on our bed. Birds out the windows.

She'll never be part of a saw palmetto
that cannot, with twenty shovels, be budged
nor has she stood with him at dusk on mud
flats, watching geese that left behind the snow.

He brought back to me a soft roseate
spoonbill feather from the marsh, a bouquet
of weeds from the roadside of his hometown.

We found a box, and in it, clothes that fit
us, we dipped our fingers into red paint,
we were no longer pots turned upside down.

III. The Dance

There was no need to turn pots upside down;
instead at my window, I watched, each day
an oak grow, then lean, still holding blue jays,
and moss winked at a mating pair of owls.

From our second story bedroom, the brown
world is a letter to not throw away,
and he is the warbler ready for play—
I'll be the wren hoping that my new sound

will last beyond the boardwalk over scrub
and beyond the pine trees that ache to crawl
toward the sky. I could become a dirt road,

or an emerald fish in an open tub,
or lie beneath the wild camphor tree. I'll
dance with him. Hold hands, even when we're old.

IV. FINAL SCENE

I'll dance, hold his hand, even when we're old
waiting in line at the store to buy cookies and milk.
The arbor we built years before will
be rotting. The bougainvillea, its bold

leaves of red, its white stamen, will have lulled
the pine tree to remain with us, but still
the gardenia never blossomed. To kill
it, I mixed its dirt with women who called

and I threw them out. I am the one in charge
of this garden. There were tears, oak trees fell
and some flowers died. There will be no more

to say about intruders to our yard.
We'll enclose the back porch. The only bell:
woodpeckers tapping words on our front door.

The Gravel Road

The only way back up this mountain
is past a tractor that long ago
stopped working and now lies on its
side, but it's the one thing noted
on a hand-drawn map: it is an object
you either turn away from
or travel past on the winding
gravel road. It is the landmark
you simply must
mention to others. Juncos
are common birds here, far
from my home. They swing
on a feeder that I cannot see
from this loft window. But there's
a model car on the window sill,
and the smell of a dead mouse
inside the wall, finally, after

five days, beginning to
dissipate. My husband who turned
too quickly lies on his side — each tiny
bone in his back eroding,
each muscle struggling to undo
the mistakes of youth
and genetics — on a mattress
downstairs that I dragged out
to the porch so he could be outside
today. And on the fireplace mantle,
I put the flowers I picked
this morning, for him, along
the side of the road, in a common
drinking glass. If I were to drive back down

the road into my childhood
and find my husband there, I'd fall
in love with him the first
time I see his face towering
above others coming toward me
in the hallway of school,
and though I would never speak
to him (even then, too worried
about saying the wrong thing)
I would not miss
a basketball game, begging God to help
him—not that he would need
it—to make more baskets than
anyone else. I would sign
my married name (his name as my own)
on the inside white pages of my
spiral notebooks,
just to watch the lines curl
and hope sing across the page. No one else
would see my future except me,
the way it would smell of rain
and how the dog barks down the mountain,
how, at times, the way to this place
has been a uneven desktop full of notes
and last names I no longer repeat.
Instead there is this cabin
where flies try to escape through closed
screens, where morning is a mirror
of mountains desperate to rise.

Atrial Fibrillation

If we stepped outside, even for a moment, we'd see
the birch-faced stars stretching
beyond the tar
of our neighbor's roof, beyond the problems
of the water pump. I suppose
it could have been a kink in the hose,
low water, guilty pots,
the money we squandered on frills
that caused the water pump to stop working,
but it was Friday,
and we would have to wait
until Monday for strangers to come
into our yard and scream at me
about how water not
coming into the house was my fault,
and so like every Friday, like hammers
pounding the house
across the street, like the separation
of concrete when tires cross a bridge,
like divisions of climates, we sat across
from each other at a restaurant, and after
the salad your words stopped and then sirens
and desperate children waiting
for the merry-go-round. On Monday I sat down
next to the purple flowers,
and instead of listening to the strange
man scream about the water pump, I thought
about how the heart monitor
mimicked crows that cross
our sky each evening. I'd stood
next to your hospital bed
and waited for the desperate
lines to become alternating posts.
I knew I could not be

your nightstand. Today, on the highway,
a plane landed. And now I rearrange
the spices waiting to bring you home.
I move them off the counter. Think of any
sound. Put up the red flag
on the mailbox. The plane was small.
Only one person killed. Others stopped
in traffic to see the small white dot. I think
of buying a sponge mop
to gather up the poison
we put down last week for roaches.
I swing just above the fear. It may take
years. The ceiling holds on. Thin bars
vibrating. Stars keep watching the purple
flowers and us and the new
water pump that we hope will last.

cerebrovascular accident

it's the end of the sky as I know it

      the blue collapsed into

   bowls of green   leaves

into dust

   on the outside of a

      window

   it's an empty cup

      a lizard carved out of stone

    near the end   of the world

all week I wait for his words   drive home

   five times each day to walk

    the dog   to watch the hanging

        pots hang in front

of my eyes   with decay

how many times have I walked

   to the cafeteria and returned

with the wrong sandwich   the wrong

cookie   his hand cannot   hold

    the doctors' names

cannot   ans

       wer back

even though green marks on the white

       board give us
            the nurse of the day

the controller of the calendar

       blocking the table

and the water I want to pour

     here's a man who can not

          speak as he once did

it is like listening to a butterfly drape the yard

     with its wings

it is like wind of an un-named storm

somewhere in the Atlantic   where all I know

are numbers on a card I carry

at all times   and instructions I wish

I did not   understand

Fighting Back

I got through it
even though the day was a collapsing

sky. This morning we waited like moths
carrying false beliefs
in our drained hands, and though
we tried to drop our fears
they slipped away from us—

we wanted to understand how only
an hour ago we sat at a table
with this new drug of sadness

and then a napkin fell
which was not unlike a river sounding its own name.

I found the scraps of summer
embedded in a skull of a long-dead frog
and now there is no time left—

or perhaps I have misplaced the entire winter.

These gusts have taken me
like a rope on the end of a thousand voices
that will never forget.

Only our voices fighting back against the flesh.

After Dinner

He tells me he wants to live alone
three weeks out of four.

Maybe absence could sound
like notes falling from clouds.

I could become the opposite
of a bench in motion.

The ladders in my room are already trying to be
something they are not.

Without stamps
envelopes want to remain where they are.

The only thing covering emptiness is paint.
In the window, clothes hang like stones.

Part V. *Toward Something*

Hope

I can't remember why I was afraid
of his old friend trying to find her way back

into his life, but it seemed longer than a minute
that I lived with curtains shredded on the window.

I could not think of how to turn the hands of his clock
back toward me. I wanted him to stare

at my breasts, to take my hands as tokens
of unlocking the only door he needed.

I wanted him to forget her name.

I have never been afraid of the woods at night,
and although I would never cut my wrists,

I want to remember the color of the kite
we flew over the field of fear for those months,

where, now, wasted hours have turned into hope.

Trapped

after Melissa Morphew, 'Sarah Frances Felt Trapped in the Noonday Light'

Dust on the floor is now a pile of leaves
beside the unused fireplace. I hover
like empty burlap in the far corner.
Light, in front of the window, is relieved.
Memory and age shred the wallpaper.
An oak has pushed itself through the cracked glass.
(I depend on that branch to be steadfast.)
The floor is speckled with grime and earth.
Years ago, someone tacked up a letter
on the wall, but I have since forgotten
what it says, and the window's skeleton
has gone limp. The only sounds: wallpaper
falling, a distant car, the leaves below,
and hopeless stories no one wants to know.

Trying to Name It

This afternoon is not quite as secretive as the katydid,
but the blue jays are attempting to scatter owls and hawks

from the yard. One day we may own a sky of sunshine,
but for now we've planted our aches and pains in sand.

Yesterday, we stood next to the stove, which is where
he mentioned the possibility of one disease that sends

us all running up trees, hiding behind leaves.
Katydids have devious ways to hide. Being born an insect

means death within days. I took his hand—why go back?
I have never been good at camouflage,

even when I'm squatting beneath a dead
tree branch, but along my walk today two old women

chatted in a driveway, and I stopped to ask the name
of the shrub in the yard, and though the owner didn't know,

she offered a clipping. The birdseed in our yard
is a sweet ad, but we have not seen

the pair of painted buntings this year, and if we knew why
stars wait light years to disappear, we'd no longer be worried.

I've watched him sleep, hiding any sign of disease
beneath the leaves of his eyes. The shrub I want to plant

in my yard is covered in flowers. The owner said it's easy
to root. It has filled her back yard with yellow. She offered

to take me there, and I wanted to know the name,
but I did not want to stop walking.

Displaced Housewife

after Betty Friedan, The Feminine Mystique

I. DISPLACEMENT

The amount of water a vessel displaces
expressed in displacement tons. But usually it is merely
the act of displacing, the state of being displaced,
or the amount or degree to which something
is displaced, as in, *I have displaced my feet,*
lost ground, can't find footing.

Physics was the first known use, in the 1600s
of displacement, and it was displacing space of one mass
by another, as in a housewife of the 1950s or 1960s exiled,
voluntarily or forced, and then she replaced her mass of a husband
with the mass of a typewriter or an order pad.

Compare Archimedes' principle which is, instead,
and thankfully came earlier—287-212 B.C., the law
that a body immersed in a fluid is buoyed up
by a buoyant force equal to the weight
of the fluid missing in the body.

And now, displacement is the linear or angular distance
in a given direction between a body
or point and a reference position. Bodies floating
in a single house or in separate houses would collide
if they were not displaced. Now we have *distance,*
the distance of an oscillating body
from its central position or point of equilibrium
at any given moment. Instead of blades on a ceiling fan
it could be four or five human bodies oscillating
from the central motor, where humming drives
all of us mad. A husband, a wife, three kids.
Like machinery, like clockwork, but specifically automotive,
displacement is the volume of the space through which

a piston travels during a single stroke in an engine
or pump. It is the total volume of the space traversed
by all the pistons, all the children sure they've
created the displacement.

ii. Exile

Prolonged separation from one's country or home
as by stress or circumstances: like wartime or a burning house
or anyone separated from his country or home voluntarily
by stress of circumstances. Work can be exile.
Expulsion from one's native land by authoritative decree
a woman who's burnt the toast too many times
or not set the plates out by the time her husband
returns from his exile of drinking at the bar with the boys.
To live in exile. A person banished from her native land:
disagreements exiled her from her family. To expel
or banish from her home/family.

The French, in 1300, created *essilier*—to drive away, as a wife
who drives away her husband if she does not
spread herself open for him. Sometimes she wanders off
voluntarily, roaming about, and in her own
way finds a place to land, or more like the Ancient Greeks
who created exile from *solum*, meaning soil, meaning where I
decide to put my own foot, how a woman walks out
of her own house, finds a different path, her own displaced soil.

The Bench Outside My Life

All these men were there — the bench filled
with regrets, the morning already turning
into crow's wings.

I was a book resting on dirt.

Perhaps I invented the men on the bench to amuse me.
Long ago, they were boys who lived through each night.

Perhaps there were other girls next to me.
Perhaps we tied bells to our feet.
Perhaps we waited too long, our dark faces toward the sky.

Toward Something

I wanted to find the pattern of yesterday
dip into that old wish but then a strange
woman speaks and it's as though I
am still waiting
on the side of a road
trying to catch a ride back
to the beginning when all I had
was a chair out on the hills
when I stood with the trees as if
I were a new day
back then
back when I was not thinking about decay
when I craved the tang of each morning
back when I was certain I'd find life
inside the house
or apples
or my voice spilling out on the sidewalk
where children have erased my footsteps
because I want to go back
find a refuge
climb the ladder toward something—
not this

Epilogue of Our Play

My life will be replayed in my complete
absence by collectors who will

very likely split every scrap, including
the inner borders of the windows that I can never

seem to clean without leaving
a streak in every pane. I'm sure they'll examine

the crust of cheese on the counter tops
where we prepared our nachos (because we never

wipe the counter entirely), and then
in the garage where even hammers were laid

gently near our bodies, as if our lives
could be distinguished from some other

married couple's cautious journey. They'll see
that we remained close to a structure

that may appear as a home (and that, finally,
we were able to walk to the paved road) but

who will care? Who will advocate
the digging up and dusting off of our entire bodies?

Who will understand that yellow leaves
on plants in the garden indicates there's not enough

iron in sand? Who will care that in this yard
a man and a woman became guardians

of each other's bodies? Will we be valuable
material in a sketch, lucky and truly

urged to become involved in
a standard argument for marriage,

or an excuse for a disobeyed rule;
will they understand the meaning of our lives?

The Empty Trail

The empty trail is an opened scarf
that carries me into the oak shadows
until the day is lost, and I am lingering
in a bed of straw and leaves.

At home, my housedress became a floating umbrella,
a memory from the heavy cart of night,
but here summer brushes my face.

I'd trade all of my wedding rings
for weeds and dirt and swamp.

I do not call on anyone's worn hands to hold me up.
I have no one to follow into the air.
Here, light opens upon vines.

Hunger is one swoop, an osprey pounding water,
and I keep walking down the long thread of the river
toward the grass of forgiveness.

www.ingramcontent.com/pod-product-compliance
Lightning Source LLC
Chambersburg PA
CBHW022038090426
42741CB00007B/1114